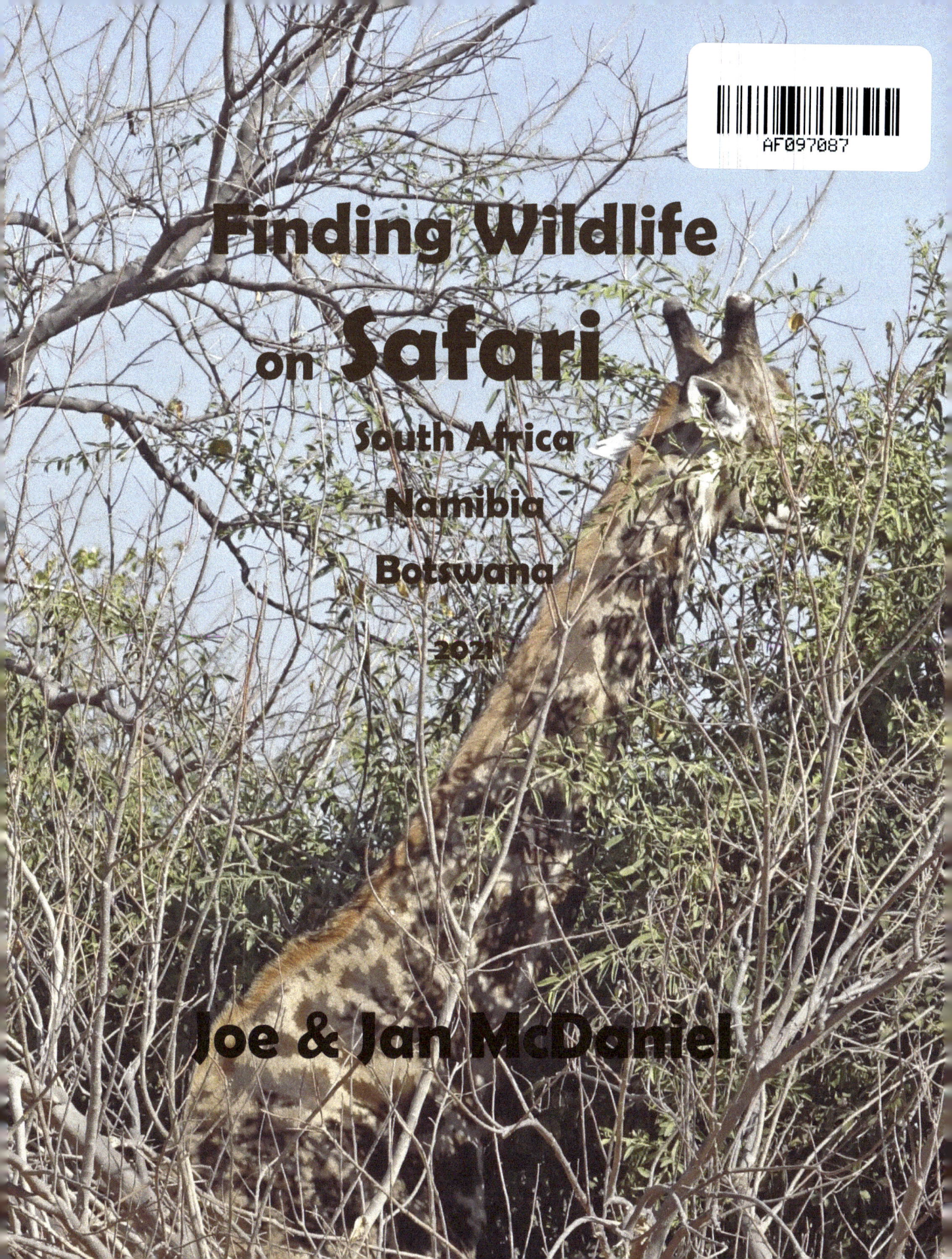

Copyright 2021 by Joe and Jan McDaniel.

Published 2021.

Printed in the United States of America.

All rights reserved.

No portion of this book may be reproduced, stored in a retrieval system, or transmitted in any form or by any means – electronic, mechanical, photocopy, recording, scanning, or other – except for brief quotations in critical reviews or articles, without the prior written permission of the authors.

ISBN 978-1-950647-94-1

Photos by Joe and Jan McDaniel

Published by BookCrafters, Parker, Colorado.
www.bookcrafters.net

# Table of Contents

Essential Safari Checklist..................................................................................................3

Photography on Safari.....................................................................................................7

Looking for Wildlife........................................................................................................11

Typical Day....................................................................................................................12

Itinerary July 24-August 16, 2021..................................................................................16

Shindzela Tented Camp, Timbavati Nature Reserve.....................................................24

Shingwedzi Rest Camp, Kruger National Park..............................................................54

Serondela Lodge, Namibia.............................................................................................87

Chobe National Park, Botswana..................................................................................106

Savuti, Chobe National Park, Botswana......................................................................121

"If there were one more thing I could do,
it would be to go on safari once again."
—Karen Blixen
(Danish author best known for "Out of Africa,"
her account of living in Kenya)

# Look how BIG Africa is

Common map projections warp our view of the globe. This graphic reveals the true size of Africa, which could fit the U.S., China, India, and more. Read More Here: https://www.visualcapitalist.com/map-true-size-of-africa/

—https://www.africa-adventure.com/countries/southern-africa-combo/

*Safari - /səˈfɑːri/ (Swahili: safari) is an overland journey to hunt or (in more recent times) observe wild animals, especially in east or southern Africa. The so-called Big Five game animals of Africa – Lion, Leopard, Rhinoceros, Elephant, and Cape Buffalo – particularly form an important part of the safari market, both for wildlife viewing and big-game hunting.*

—Webster's Dictionary

Often we are asked why we return to Africa time and again. Africa is an enormous continent with so many varied destinations—some we return to and others to explore a first time. On safari one never knows what they might encounter over the next rise or around the next bend in the road. The anticipation of sighting wildlife is addictive, and even if a game drive doesn't fulfill expectations, the scenery, the smell, and the sounds of the bush are amazing. The colors of the sky from dawn till dusk alone are worth the trip. The melodic cooing of the doves, the harrumph of the Hippo and the whoop of the Hyena remind us why we return.

A safari is the most unusual experience there is—we seldom encounter a first-time visitor who does not want to return. Whether you are traveling to Africa for the first time, or returning, each trip is unique.

"But aren't you afraid?" we are asked. "We are afraid we'll eat too much," we reply. The food is plentiful and delicious: rich creamy soups, grilled meats, game and fish, yummy vegetables, salads, tropical fruits and delicious puddings for dessert. Restaurant fare is varied and reasonable. American fast food such as KFC, McDonalds and pizza are often available in larger towns.

Hospitality is the backbone of many African country's economies. Tourists are warmly welcomed with a willingness to do anything to make their stay comfortable and memorable. Licensed game guides tirelessly answer questions and make every effort to help photographers capture the best pictures. They communicate by radio with other guides when rare wildlife is spotted so other visitors can share in the sighting. Trackers may walk alone through the bush in search of The Big Five or the elusive Wild Dog den. The camp staff meets every request with a smile. Laundry is removed and returned neatly folded the same day.

Renting a vehicle to self-drive in national parks is a good option. Be certain to ask for the best vehicle for your itinerary—sometimes 4-wheel drive is necessary—or a mid-size sedan will be adequate and comfortable. Campers are also available for hire. These arrangements can be made well in advance on the Internet.

Accommodations and camp sites in national park rest camps are clean, comfortable, and available for a couple or families for nominal fees. Visitors can purchase groceries in nearby towns or camp stores or eat in camp restaurants. Laundromats are located in camping area in major parks. Most roads are well maintained and signage, in English, is helpful. However, be sure to have maps of the country and park(s) you are visiting. If you are uncertain about driving in a national park, guided tours and game drives are available for hire.

A multitude of rest camps offer a wide variety of price points. You can self-drive safely in the national parks or be whisked away from an airport by a driver to a private game reserve. If you want a spa/golf experience, those are available as well. Camping facilities with ablutions are abundant and well-maintained, and B&Bs and self-catering bungalows are available in national parks and nearby towns. Or you can participate in a guided camping safari with friendly competent staff to attend to your every need. An experienced travel agent can help you plan your trip of a lifetime. However, amazing wildlife can be seen from any camp. Several game camps may share the same areas, so keep that in mind when considering costs and which facility to book.

Depending on the season, malaria may be a factor in some areas. In most places you can drink the local water and eat anything offered in restaurants. You will be advised if water is not potable. We do not get inoculations (yellow fever, hepatitis, etc.) for traveling in southern Africa, but check with your physician or the CDC for guidance.

This book contains some suggestions and guidelines for a safari. Tour companies will provide a lot of detailed information, but we offer some first-hand advice from our own African travel experiences over the last twenty-five years. We have just returned from three weeks in South Africa, Namibia and Botswana during the COVID19 pandemic and share our adventures in the following pages.

# ESSENTIAL SAFARI CHECK LIST

- **PASSPORT** – Make sure your passport will remain valid for at lease six months after your return from your trip. Passports should have at least two blank pages for customs and immigration stamps.

- **CAMERA** – We travel with several cameras: two mirrorless Sony Alpha 6000 cameras, one with a 16-50mm lens and the other with a Sony 70-350mm zoom lens. We used a small point-and-shoot camera for quick memory shots (one could use their phone for these photos). A Sony Digital HD video camera recorder was used for action shots and a Browning Trail Camera (Model No. BTC-7A) captured some videos as well. We combine videos of each trip, usually thirty seconds to one minute in duration, for a video journal.

- **SPARE BATTERIES AND CHARGER** – Be certain to have spare batteries with you when on a game drive. All game camps will have charging stations. Most safari vehicles will have USB charging ports on-board.

- **POWER CONVERTER** – A three round-pin adapter is used in South Africa. Other countries may require different adapters to charge your batteries. Adapters are available for purchase in airports or from many online stores.

- **FLASHLIGHT (TORCH)** – Once the sun goes down it quickly becomes dark and camp tents/bungalows are a short walk from the main lodge. It is best to have your own flashlight.

- **SATELLITE PHONE** – If you don't have a SIM card for international calls, your phone may not connect in Africa. We travel with an international phone which is very useful. You can purchase or rent an international phone on the Internet. Mobile phones can also be rented or purchased at international airports. However, keep in mind that international flights from the USA and Europe often arrive in the evening and stores at airports may not be open.

- **MAPS** – (Tinkers™ Maps and Guides for southern African countries) Even if you are not self-driving, maps are great references for general information, wildlife checklists, phone numbers, activities, and estimating driving distances. We were grateful for National Park contact numbers found in our Tinkers™ Tourist Map when we needed assistance. Maps may be purchased in airports or national park camp stores.

- **PEN AND NOTEBOOK** - Keep a pen and small notebook on hand to complete forms. We use a 5x7-inch hard-back folder to hold yellow pads for notes. Often there is a queue, and no surface to write on when required to fill out immigration forms, on arrival and departure from each country. Each day Jan wrote her notes here for reference when writing this book.

- **QUICK REFERENCE OF CONTACT INFORMATION** - Make a list of the following for each traveler for quick reference when completing forms. We wished we had made a list of the following as we needed this information repeatedly.
    o   Date of birth for each member of your group
    o   Nationality (USA)
    o   Passport number and expiration date for each person
    o   Country of origin (where you are transferring from—US, South Africa, Botswana, etc.)
    o   Date of arrival/departure
    o   City and/or country traveling to
    o   Flight/vessel/vehicle number
    o   Seat number/s
    o   Telephone at destination in country (including country code)
    o   Email address for each person
    o   Physical address at destination (home, hotel, lodge or camp name)
    o   Contact cell phone number
    o   Emergency contact name and phone number (next of kin)
    o   Rental car registration number
    o   Local address (hotel/lodge)

- **MONEY** - SMALL DENOMINATIONS OF US DOLLARS - Take fifty to seventy-five $1 and $5 dollar bills for tips at airports, restaurants, etc. Larger denominations of money ($50 and $100) are useful for tips for game guides and camp staff. We generally tip $10 per person per day (minimum) for game guides and trackers, and $5 per day for support staff. US dollars are accepted for tips as the exchange rate (at present) is greater than local currency. Credit cards (Visa and MasterCard) are widely accepted when Wi-Fi is working.
    o   Small local currency coins to pay for use of public toilets in some locations (we did not need it this time, but have on other trips)

- **WARM CLOTHES** – Be aware that seasons are opposite from the US, so if you are traveling in June, July or August, it is winter in southern Africa. It can get very cold; one night it was 35°F. Take a warm coat, scarf, hat, gloves, and/or hoodie-fleece jacket to wear on game drives in open vehicles. Pack warm pajamas. Dress in layers for game drives because when the sun rises, it warms up quickly, and we took off our heavy coats and were comfortable in just a fleece jacket.
    - However, even though it is winter in those months, pack shorts and short sleeve shirts as it can be very warm during the day.
    - Comfortable shoes for walking in dirt and sand. Game camps do not have paved sidewalks.
    - Put a fleece jacket or hoodie in your carry-on to wear on the plane if necessary—we were glad we did.
    - You do not need to purchase "safari attire." Just pack ordinary clothes suitable for the season. Rarely will you see the local residents wearing the "Out of Africa" safari styles favored by many American travelers.
- **CLOTH BAG** – A small cloth bag was handy to carry bottled water or pack away scarves and other items when on game drives.
- **COPIES OF PHOTO PAGE OF PASSPORT**, DRIVERS LICENSE, BOOKING CONFIRMATIONS – Keep copies of personal documents in a separate place from the originals.
- **LEAVE WITH FAMILY OR FRIENDS** - Copies of your itinerary and contact information.
- **MISCELLANEOUS ITEMS** – Sunglasses, sunscreen, insect repellent, hand sanitizer, toilet paper (at times toilet paper is not available in public toilets—so it is best to be prepared), tissues, zip lock bags, first-aid kit, binoculars, bird and mammal guidebooks, face cloth (only hand and bath towels are provided in accommodations), book to read (we take several paperback books that we leave behind when read).

**AFRICAN CUSTOMS** – Shops may close at noon on Saturday and are not open Sunday. Check school and holiday schedules online before booking your safari as local residents crowd national parks on school holidays and accommodations may not be available.
- Hot water is often on the right hand rather than the left as in the US. Some camps use solar power, so it may be best to shower mid-day or evening to ensure you have hot water.
- National Park camp restaurants do not open before the sun rises, so if you want breakfast before you leave on an early game drive, eat some cereal in your bungalow.
- Gates in National Parks open at sunrise and close at sunset.

**SUGGESTION** - Spend at least three nights in each location. To enjoy the complete safari experience, it is best to stay in one place three or more nights. Do not waste vacation time traveling between camps every other day.

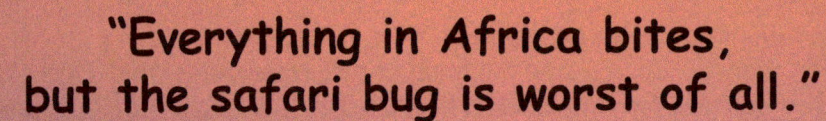

"Everything in Africa bites,
but the safari bug is worst of all."
—Brian Jackman
(British journalist and author, best known for his interest
in wildlife and wild places – especially Africa)

# PHOTOGRAPHY on SAFARI

In this age of digital photography, anyone can take a good photo with a mobile phone. To take good wildlife photographs however, one needs a good (not necessarily expensive) camera that can be adjusted to suit the conditions of the moment—sensitivity, focus, aperture (exposure), zoom, etc.

Often, those who use their phones to take photos will keep those images on their phone and not download them to a computer. We take photographs so we can publish a travel journal of each trip, so downloading all images and saving them on a thumb drive or laptop is very important to us.

There are many good cameras on the market today. The most important thing is to have a good, dependable camera body and to choose a zoom lens, sized to suit the conditions you will experience. I have been asked if one needs a 400mm telephoto lens in Africa. My answer is, "If you are photographing Elephant, you might only need a 70mm lens, because they are very big, and you will be very close!"

However, if you are interested in photographing birds, then a bigger lens is obviously necessary.

I have settled on Sony Mirrorless cameras. They are very lightweight, very compact, and have all the features needed to photograph wildlife in a variety of conditions. They also have one of the fastest auto focus features in the business. Sony Mirrorless cameras range in price up to US$6,000. My Alpha 6000 cameras cost $400 to $500, and each one has a 24.7 Mega Pixel sensor.

I also have two identical camera bodies for several reasons. 1) If one camera is damaged then I have a backup. 2) With two different lenses, there is never a need to switch a lens while traveling. Lens bayonet fittings are sensitive and can wear out from repeated use. 3) My camera with the 16-50mm lens is useful for local pictures (airports, hotel interiors, people, sunsets!) that don't require a telephoto. At times we become so engrossed in taking wildlife pictures that we forget to record the other, in-between, experiences of our journey.

Many questions about digital cameras, of all brands, can be answered at Digital Camera World at https://www.digitalcameraworld.com/.

The Sony E 70-350mm f/4.5-6.3 G OSS zoom lens is designed specifically for APS-C format Sony E-mount cameras and sports a 5x zoom range equating to 105-525mm on a full-frame body. And it very light-weight.

Sony also offers free online editing software that is very versatile and easy-to-use for formatting both photos and videos. Amateur photographers, who may not be familiar with Photoshop, will find this software very helpful. Other camera brands will offer similar software for their products.

We also take a Sony HDR-CX405 Full HD Handycam Camcorder video camera with us (purchased for less than US$300). This is small and lightweight, fits in our one camera bag, and allows us to take some great video recordings. A small, lightweight tripod to keep our video recordings steady is useful. For active subjects, such as a herd of Elephants swimming across a river, or Lions on a kill, this records great memories of our trips. Although it is often tempting to record for several minutes or more, we generally edit these and trim them to thirty seconds to a minute in length.

Finally, we have a Sony Pocket-sized camera. The newer model (DSC-W830 Digital Camera from Sony is a pocket-sized point-and-shoot featuring a 20.1MP image sensor) is available for about US$130. This is extremely convenient and useful when your other cameras are in the aircraft overhead or in your backpack and can't be reached. Picture quality is excellent, and this is perfect for those people-pictures in informal settings—say, around the campfire or at a restaurant.

## No matter your photography skill level, here are some important things to remember:

- **The Golden Rule** – Never go anywhere without a camera on hand.
- Read your camera instruction booklet and practice making adjustments before your trip. Practice taking photographs at home and become familiar with all important features of your equipment.
- <u>Read the instructions again</u>, and take a copy of the camera manual with you.
- Learn the importance of being able to control
    o the ISO (sensitivity)
    o the aperture (F-stop)
    o the shutter speed.

- **ISO** is the name of the International Organization of Standardization: a body that creates thousands of agreed standards for a huge range of products, procedures, and practices. For the photographer, ISO is simply a set of numbers, but an important tool.

  —https://www.digitalcameraworld.com/tutorials

- The **F-stop** (aperture) is the most important setting to understand and control for getting the best "depth-of-field" in your images. Depth of field is a measure of how much of a picture is in focus. By adjusting the F-stop to its lowest number (say F5.4 or F6.1) on your camera you can, for example, focus on a bird and have the background blurred or out of focus. If focusing on larger subjects, set the F-stop to a high number (say F22) to ensure that everything in the picture, foreground, the subject, and background are all in focus.

- **Shutter Speed** dictates how long the camera's sensor is exposed to light. Find out what shutter speeds are best for different subject matter. For a motionless animal you can use 1/125ths sec, but for a bird in flight you will want a higher speed of 1/2500ths sec to freeze the detail of the moving wings.

- Make sure you have enough batteries and take a compact battery or camera charger with you. In some locations there may not be electrical outlets available for a day or two, so you want to have batteries in reserve. Be prepared.

- It may go without saying, but be sure you take the necessary charging cables with USB connections and adapters. Most rental cars today will have USB outlets, but they are useless unless you can connect them to your devices.

- Learn how to clean your camera lenses and sensors to eliminate spots and specks from your photographs. Small, compact cleaning kits are available online or from camera stores.

- Set the date and time for each camera to the local time zone as soon as you arrive in the foreign country. This is <u>very important and often neglected</u>. Remember, each photo you take, and save in a folder, will have the date and exact time-taken on it. (Right click on the image icon and this will pop up.)

- Having an accurate record of when each photo was taken is always very helpful when putting together a diary of your experiences. The photos ensure you can piece together an accurate timeline.

- While on safari **always** <u>**pre-adjust**</u> your camera settings to anticipate local conditions. This saves critical seconds when a photo opportunity suddenly happens. And they often "suddenly" happen! For example: when leaving camp in the early morning, sometimes before the sun is up, adjust your camera for low-light conditions by increasing the ISO (camera sensitivity setting) to compensate.

- As soon as you see conditions change—e.g., when the sun is up! – make another adjustment. Always try to anticipate what may happen next.

- Save your photos on a laptop or on a thumb drive in folders. Tag each photo with an appropriate, but brief, caption. (Right click on the photo icon, then select "rename").
- As with any kind of photography, it is helpful to "know your subject matter." If you are making your first trip to Africa, we suggest you review descriptions of the birds, mammals, and other wildlife that you will encounter. Often you may take a picture of a bird that you can't identify at the time, but a photo will make it easier to find later in a reference book, and then you can caption the photo correctly. Correct animal identification is important. We have heard a Guinea Fowl referred to as a "Spotted Chicken." Amusing but inexcusable.
- Include pictures of road signs, notices, and descriptive wording on buildings, etc. in your shots. These will come in handy when recalling your experiences, spelling foreign words and names correctly, and getting your history right.
- Keep in mind that you don't have to take photographs to match those in glossy travel magazines. Your photos should record **your personal experiences**. Be realistic.

# LOOKING FOR WILDLIFE

Wildlife and birds are everywhere in Africa. Warthog, Impala or Baboon, may be seen when you land on the runway in the bush or even roaming in towns. When game crosses the road in front of the vehicle it is easy to see, however, if you <u>actively look</u> for it, you will be amazed at what is behind a bush or up a tree.

When on a game drive in an open vehicle with a licensed game guide driver and tracker, they will search for the wildlife. The tracker sits on the front left fender of the vehicle looking for spoor (tracks), and with his trained eyes scans left and right to find the animals. He indicates to the driver to stop, and the driver tells passengers where to look.

But you should also be looking side to side, up and down, front and back. Wildlife is camouflaged for a reason—to make it difficult to see! An Elephant can be standing beside the road feeding, and unless you are really looking and listening, you may not see it. Horns on antelope may at first look like the branch of a tree, especially when the animal stands perfectly still... So train your eyes and ears as you scan your surroundings to see or hear some movement, the twitch of an ear, the flash of a tail, antelope running, a rumble of noise, the loud chatter of Guinea Fowl or Baboons.

Often wildlife is easy to spot and photograph. Lions generally sleep during the day unless they are feeding on a kill, so they may be lying in the shade of a bush or in the tall grass—watch for a tail waving. Bull Elephants are often alone or in groups of three. Breeding herds of mothers and babies sometimes walk single file or browse for food in groups of large numbers with older Elephants surrounding the young. Leopards will pull their kill into a tree to eat, so look up and you may be fortunate to find one. Buffalo are often close to water and in large herds, the old males are outcasts and may be lying in a pool of muddy water. These are called "Dagga boys." Rhinos are bulky but shy and don't often pose for pictures.

Hippos bob up and down in water with only ears, eyes and nose showing—now you see them, now you don't—or lie close together on the bank. Giraffe can be seen looking over the top of a tree, and seldom is there just one. The Hyena and the Black-backed Jackal are often spotted near a kill waiting their turn to clean up the scraps.

Raptors and colorful birds will be in the open on a bare branch. Vultures soar in circles or rest in trees. Guinea Fowl, Spurfowl and Francolin run along the road, but the tiny Bee-eaters and Kingfishers are more difficult to find. Crocodiles sun on the banks of rivers and Water Monitors waddle around as well.

Impala are everywhere, sometimes in large herds or just a few bachelors hanging out together. Zebra are usually in groups and dash quickly across a road. Waterbuck have a round target on their rumps and will be near water. Majestic Kudu with spiral horns can be found deep in the bush watching you from behind a thorn tree. Nyala can been seen in thickets and dry woodland. Tiny Steenboks stay by roadsides and Klipspringers hop from rock to rock high on kopjes. We were really lucky to see the less common Sable and Roan antelope.

## TYPICAL DAY

A typical day is like the one below, although the timetable isn't set if a game sighting keeps you longer. The sound of a drum will alert you when it is time to eat, and a staff member will announce the fare for that meal. We were given a menu at Shindzela to let us choose breakfast and dinner selections in advance. The times shown here are for winter. As summer days are longer, times will vary slightly.

|  |  |
|---|---|
| 6:00 a.m. | wake-up call, before sunrise |
| 6:30 a.m. | meet at lodge for coffee/tea and a rusk |
| 6:45 a.m. | climb into the Land Cruiser for the morning game drive |
| 8:00 a.m. | stop in the bush for coffee and muffins, leg stretch, and bush toilet (squat behind a bush or the vehicle, take along a small plastic bag for the toilet paper) |
| 10:00 a.m. | return to camp for breakfast (buffet: fruit, yogurt, cereals, and cooked breakfast: eggs, toast, sausage, bacon, mushrooms, tomato) |
| 10:30 - 2:00 | free time in camp or walk with a guide in the bush |
| 2:00 p.m. | lunch in the lodge (a filling light meal such as: chicken wrap, quiche, babootie, pasta salad) |
| 2:30 - 3:30 | free time in camp |
| 3:30 p.m. | afternoon game drive |

| | |
|---|---|
| 5:30 p.m. | stop in the bush for sundowners (drinks and snacks) and enjoy stunning African sunsets |
| 6:00 – 7:00 | night-drive back to camp (tracker looks for game with bright spotlight) |
| 7:15 p.m. | dinner in the boma near the fire (soup and/or salad with bread starter, main course meat, starch and vegetables, dessert: pudding or cake or fruit crisp |
| 8:00 p.m. | remain by fire to recount the day or go to bed |

Be sure to spend at least three nights in a game camp when staying in a private game reserve. This offers the true safari experience. There are many options to choose from for the type of camp, permanent en-suite tents on raised platforms, or thatch-roofed bungalows with air conditioning, around a main lodge and swimming pool. Meals, accommodation, park fees, game drives and walks are included in the price of the stay. Coffee and tea, and sometimes hot chocolate, are available 24/7 at no charge, but soft drinks and alcohol are an extra charge. Most private camps have Wi-Fi and charging stations for batteries.

In the Klaserie and Timbavati Private Game Reserves, adjacent to the Kruger National Park, game guides can drive off-road for an up-close look at Lions or a Wild Dog den. The tracker may walk through the bush and radio the driver where to find the game. Guides from other camps in the area communicate by radio to share viewing experiences or search for animals.

Meals are plentiful and delicious—you won't go hungry—and are sometimes served in a boma (an outdoor native pole enclosure) around a roaring fire. Guests can have their laundry done for a nominal fee. Some more expensive camps have exercise rooms and spa facilities, but the game drives may be in the area that is shared with less expensive camps or lodges.

When on game drives, the guide will stop as close to the wildlife as possible with the sun positioned best for photographs, turn off the engine, and quietly answer questions or talk about the animal habits or characteristics. They'll share native stories and legends. These well-trained and qualified guides are very knowledgeable and can identify hundreds of birds and every creature great and small. Sometimes your vehicle will be the only one at a sighting. One can learn a great deal about the wildlife and the local environment from these guides.

The thrill of seeing your first Elephant, Giraffe or the rare Wild (Painted) Dog is indescribable. It will be a memory you will never forget. On the following pages we'll share some of our experiences and photographs in a private game camp in the Timbavati Game Reserve, self-driving in Kruger National Park, cruising on the Chobe River from a private lodge, and self-driving in Chobe National Park.

*Wildlife is often camouflaged in the bush. LOOK carefully and you may see...*

You won't go hungry!

# ITINERARY July 24-August 16, 2021

We flew from Denver, Colorado to Newark, New Jersey where we boarded a Boeing 787 plane for a 15-hour direct flight to Johannesburg, South Africa. We had been tested (PCR test) for COVID19 within 72-hours of our flight and had to show the test results before boarding the plane. It was very cold on the plane, so we were glad we had fleece jackets and hoodies. We were required to wear face masks in airports and on the planes. Drinks, dinner, and breakfast were served, and some snacks were available. Each seat had a screen to watch movies, TV programs or the flight plan of the plane. We took prescription sleeping pills and slept for a few hours.

Upon arrival in Jo'burg, we went through immigration, collected our luggage, and caught the shuttle bus to an airport hotel. It was very cold outside and in our room. After a restless night and early breakfast, we returned to the airport. Our fifty-five-minute flight was on a prop jet, with only five other passengers, to Eastgate Airport near Hoedspruit, South Africa.

We had an extra day, due to a flight change (not enough passengers due to COVID19), so we rented a car and booked a night at **Call of the Wild Lodge** in the **Hoedspruit Wildlife Estate**. Our well-appointed room and gracious hosts gave us a chance to relax and regroup. The estate is home to antelope, Giraffe, Zebra, Warthog, and many colorful birds, so we whetted our appetite for our safari with a game drive that afternoon. Residents and visitors may safely walk through the reserve among the wildlife.

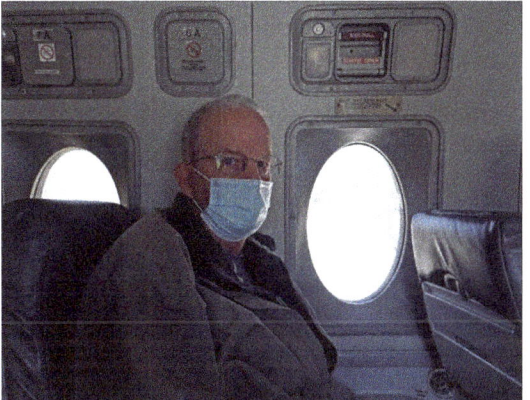

Vacant waiting room at OR Tambo International Airport

CemAir flight with seven passengers

    The **Hoedspruit Wildlife Estate** is a conserved area with a reserve that is home to a fabulous array of plants and animals. Impala and Kudu graze peacefully, while stocky Warthogs keep their noses close to the ground in search of roots and tubers to eat.

    More than 200 hectares (494 acres) of pristine Lowveld bush is dedicated to these animals, as well as to a host of bird and insect species. Visitors are encouraged to bring their binoculars, and to keep an eye out for the exciting avian species that call this home.

    The town of Hoedspruit is small and charming, with incredible views of the Drakensberg Mountains as an idyllic backdrop. It is also home to a number of shops and restaurants, adding to its convenience for visitors from around the world.

—https//www.sa-venues.com/game-reserves/hoedspruit-wildlife-estate.php

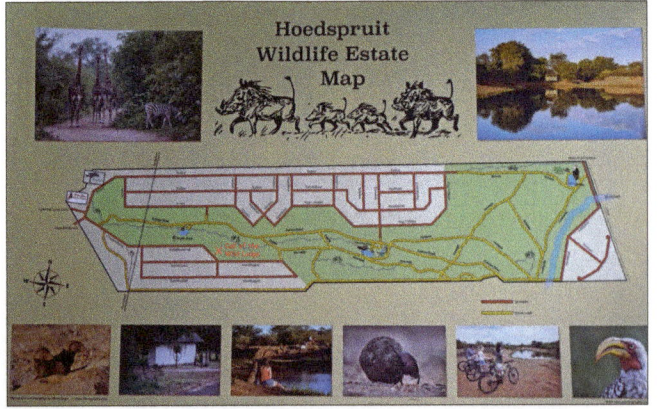

Yellow-billed Hornbill

Female Lesser-masked Weaver

Grey Go-away Bird

Nyala ram

Male Lesser Masked Weaver

Blue Wildebeest

Crested Franklin

Greater Blue Starling

Red-billed Hornbill

Speckled Mousebird

Bushbaby

Common or Grey Duiker

Female Waterbuck

Male Waterbuck

Baby female Giraffe

A "Tower" of Giraffe

Jan in **Call of the Wild** garden

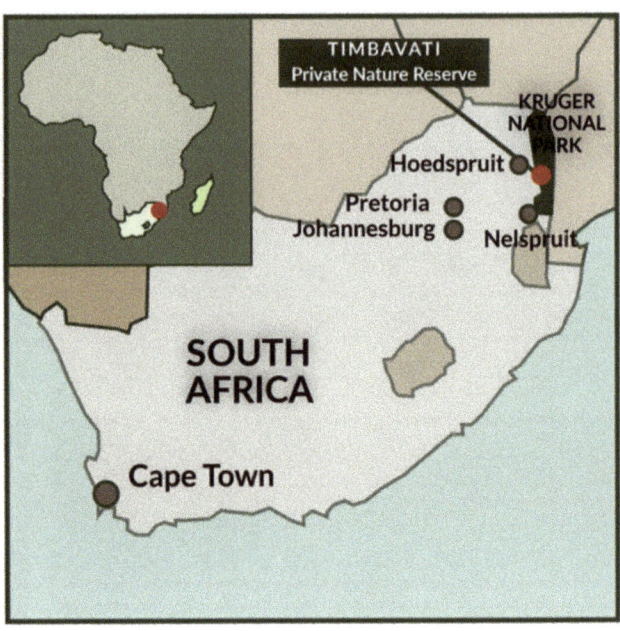

# TIMBAVATI PRIVATE RESERVE, SOUTH AFRICA

The Timbavati Private Nature Reserve, over 53 000 hectares (131,000 acres) of unspoilt natural wilderness. The Timbavati Private Nature Reserve lies within the Greater Kruger National Park open system, and within the internationally declared Kruger 2 Canyons UNESCO Man and Biosphere System. These systems, in turn, fall within the Great Limpopo Transfrontier Conservation Area (GLTFCA), a truly visionary landscape of reserves and habitats working together under a common agreement signed between 3 countries (South Africa, Mozambique and Zimbabwe) in 2002. Together these reserves occupy 184,000 hectares (710 square miles) of land which is dedicated to wildlife.

—https://timbavati.co.za/

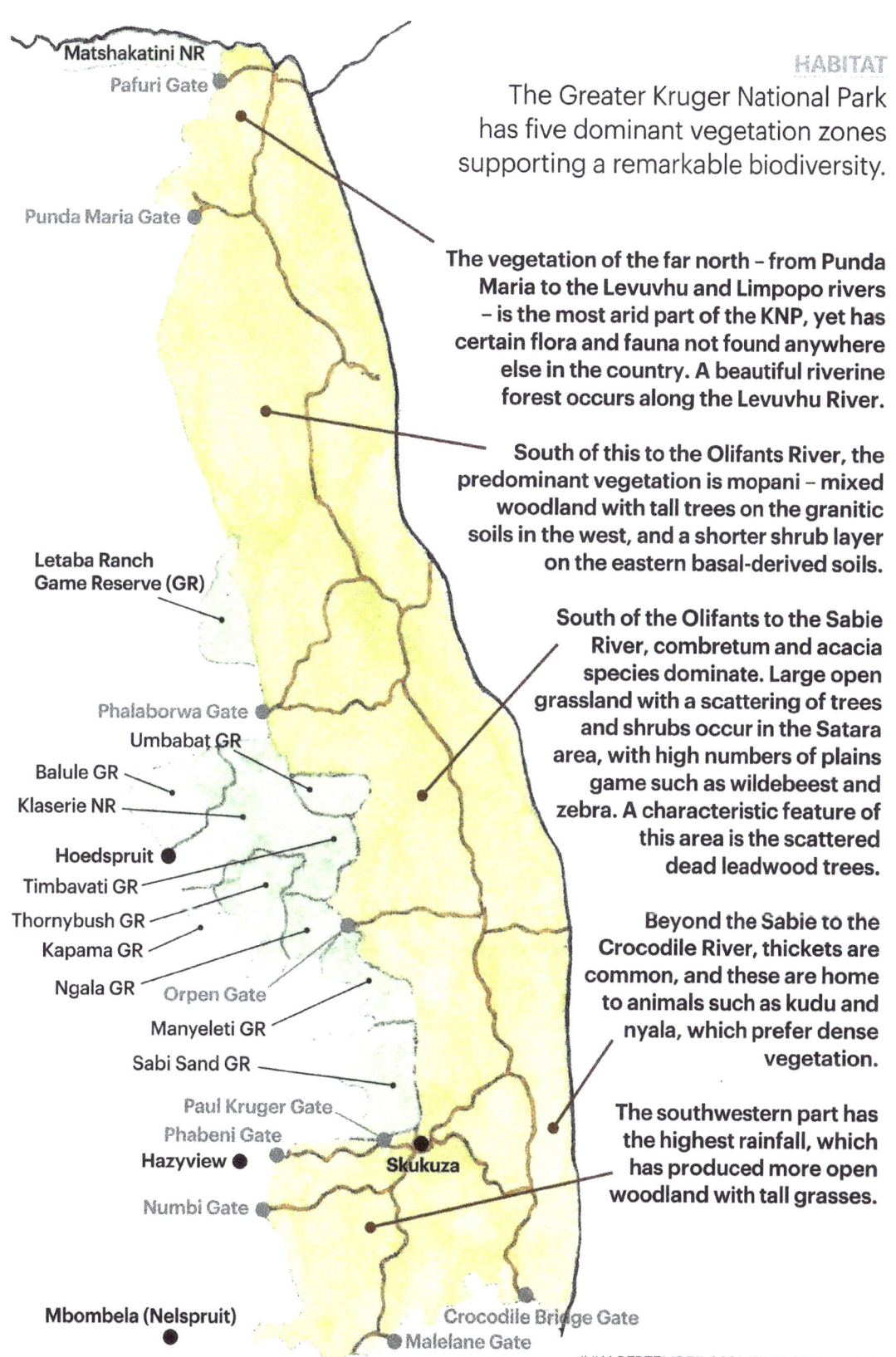

### HABITAT

The Greater Kruger National Park has five dominant vegetation zones supporting a remarkable biodiversity.

The vegetation of the far north – from Punda Maria to the Levuvhu and Limpopo rivers – is the most arid part of the KNP, yet has certain flora and fauna not found anywhere else in the country. A beautiful riverine forest occurs along the Levuvhu River.

South of this to the Olifants River, the predominant vegetation is mopani – mixed woodland with tall trees on the granitic soils in the west, and a shorter shrub layer on the eastern basal-derived soils.

South of the Olifants to the Sabie River, combretum and acacia species dominate. Large open grassland with a scattering of trees and shrubs occur in the Satara area, with high numbers of plains game such as wildebeest and zebra. A characteristic feature of this area is the scattered dead leadwood trees.

Beyond the Sabie to the Crocodile River, thickets are common, and these are home to animals such as kudu and nyala, which prefer dense vegetation.

The southwestern part has the highest rainfall, which has produced more open woodland with tall grasses.

# SHINDZELA TENTED CAMP

The following day we returned to the nearby **Eastgate Airport**, where we were met by a driver to take us to **Shindzela Tented Camp** in the **Timbavati Private Nature Reserve**, our home for the next five nights. We were greeted by our game guide and camp manager Brett Marneweck and shown to our tent accommodation with a view of a water hole. It was sad to learn we were the only people in the eight-tent camp for our stay. Needless to say, we had VIP treatment. Jenneth beat the drum for meals and served us. Lunch was served in the main lodge, a large open, thatched roofed structure, and we had time to settle in before our first game drive that afternoon.

Jeffery, a tracker we had on a previous trip in another camp, was reintroduced. We told Jeffrey we wanted to see a Leopard in a tree and Wild Dogs—a big order since both are quite rare. We took our seats in the Land Cruiser with cameras at the ready and drove off into the Mopani woodlands bush. Within thirty minutes we stopped beneath a tangled tree where a male Leopard was perched above us with the carcass of an Impala. A second Leopard sneaked through the bush close by, and Hyena paced around in the tall grass. Wild Dogs were in the area, and we saw them running on the hunt for their evening meal. What thrills and photographic moments! Our safari had truly begun.

We returned to camp for dinner in the boma by the fire under a million stars: Greek salad, potato soup, fresh bread, pork chops, sweet potatoes, green beans and carrots, and peppermint pudding. It was very cold, and we were grateful to find hot water bottles at the foot of our bed. We put the extra warm blanket beneath the sheet and comforter next to our bodies which helped keep us warm. Hyenas whooped during the night and birds greeted the new day. We were awake early and ready to continue our adventure.

In the following days we explored different areas of the Timbavati Reserve in search of game. We stopped by waterholes and dams to watch Hippo and Elephant, we bushwhacked through the bush after spotting a Leopard, but she disappeared. There were Giraffe, Rhino, Buffalo and Kudu, and of course hundreds of Impala. We even saw two African Wildcats and an African Civet in the spotlight one night returning to camp.

Lions! Yes, we saw Lions. They would hardly raise their heads to look at us the first time we saw them sleeping cuddled together. But the following morning the eight young males were on the move, and we watched them emerge from the shadowy bush near our vehicle. Their size is enormous—no wonder they are called "king of the beasts."

But the highlight of the game viewing in this area was a pack of thirteen Wild Dogs with eleven puppies. Brett took us to a den the dogs had abandoned, and then he and Jeffrey tracked them to another area. They left us in the vehicle and walked into the bush. It was so quiet until we heard yipping. Jeffrey and Brett came running back and we drove off-road through tall grass and over thorny bushes to a large termite mound where we found the puppies running and playing, chewing on tails, trying to steal a stick, and just being adorable puppies. The adults sleeping here and there occasionally interacted with the pups. It was a once-in-a-lifetime sighting, so rare. For over an hour we sat alone in the bush surrounded by Wild Dogs. As we left, the adults got up and went onto the road. We followed them to a dam where they lapped a long drink before spreading out to hunt. Then they ran and ran through the bush, and we raced along the road spotting a white-tipped tail here and there until they disappeared. Breathtaking.

We really enjoyed our time at Shindzela, a camp we had wanted to visit for several years. The Grey Go-away Bird told us to "go-away," but we hated to leave. Not only was the game viewing fantastic—Elephants at the camp waterhole while we had lunch one day—but the meals were superb: lamb chops, ostrich steak, stuffed chicken breasts, milk tart (a favorite), chocolate mousse, apple crisp, yummy!

Shindela Tented Camp tent and lodge - Jenneth (below)

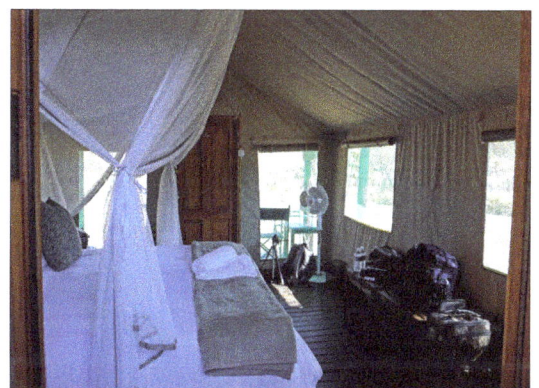

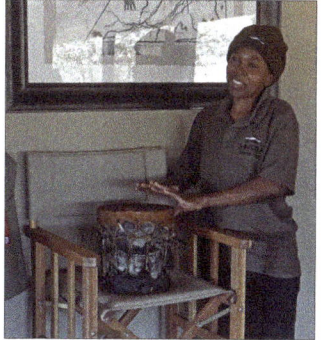

Our guide Brett and tracker Jeffrey

Early morning game drive

We leave camp before sunrise for a game
drive and stop for a coffee break in the morning.
In the evening it's time for sundowners.
We get close to the wildlife for photographs.

Leopard in a tree with a kill. Another Leopard and a Hyena roam down below.

Leopard

Wild Dogs on the hunt

Wild Dog puppy

Frisky, adorable Wild Dog puppies

A Cape Buffalo herd comes to drink - Old "Dagga" boy (below)

Yellow-billed Oxpeckers groom Cape Buffalo for parasites
Buffalo on the road in the Timbavati Reserve

After sunset, dinner by the fire in the boma

Elephants drink at the dam and we drive close for a good look

Male Lions

The elusive Leopard disappeared in the tall grass

Impala, Wildebeest and Giraffe

Steenbok female

Waterbuck ewe

Waterbuck at the dam

Hippo

This zebra is missing its tail

White-backed Vulture and nest

White Rhino

Black-backed Jackal

Look at the tusks on this Warthog

Kudu cow and Kudu bull

Wild Dogs

Wild Dog puppies (above) - Adults on the hunt (below)

You never know what may be on the road ahead

Steenbok hiding from Wild Dogs

Baby Hippo on mother's back

Buffalo

Spider web

Hyena in the spotlight

White Rhino

Hyena at dusk

Saddle-billed Stork

Lilac-breasted Roller with insect

Bateleur Eagle

Red-crested Korhaan

Verreaux's Eagle Owl (left and above)

Lions on the move near us

# KRUGER NATIONAL PARK (KNP), SOUTH AFRICA

The Kruger National Park is one of the largest game reserves in Africa. It extends across the Limpopo and Mpumalanga provinces of South Africa, reaching to the border with Zimbabwe in the north and Mozambique in the east. In 1898 it was known as the Government Wildlife Park; later it became the Sabi Game Reserve and in 1926, the Kruger National Park. Where nearly 2 million hectares (7,720 square miles) of unrivaled diversity of life forms fuses with historical and archaeological sites —this is real Africa. The world-renowned Kruger National Park offers a wildlife experience that ranks with the best in Africa.

1. All accommodation, ablution and kitchen facilities are serviced by cleaning staff on a daily basis.
2. Day visitors will no longer be allowed to bring or consume alcohol in public areas such as parking lots, picnic sites, wildlife viewing areas or roads, gates and all other areas designated as public.
3. As outdoor lighting in camps is limited, a torch/headlamp is required when walking outside at night.
4. Most rest-camps have retail facilities and restaurants. Tariff prices do not include meals.
5. Plan your trip - do not try and cover too great a distance. The Kruger National Park is a massive tract of land and frequently visitors try to cover too much ground. Slow travel and regular stopping produces much more action than covering a lot of ground.
6. Early mornings and evening time are usually the most productive game viewing periods.

—https://www.sanparks.org/parks/kruger/

Shingwedzi chalet in KNP

# SHINGWEDZI REST CAMP

Our next destination was four nights in a bungalow at **Shingwedzi Rest Camp** in **Kruger National Park**. It was warmer in this area. We picked up our AVIS rental car at the Hoedspruit Airport and purchased a few groceries at the Pick n Pay Supermarket in town before driving north to the town of Phalaborwa. The best part of self-drive is you can decide where to go and how long to stay. After an overnight stay and breakfast at **Bothabelo B&B**, we drove the short distance to the Phalaborwa Gate into Kruger National Park. We saw Elephant, Wild Dogs (again!) and Buffalo before arriving at camp. There were not many occupied bungalows (due to the COVID situation), but many campers.

Our comfortable air-conditioned bungalow had a table and chairs, microwave, cooktop and kitchen utensils on the covered porch. The refrigerator was inside because Baboons can open them and steal the contents. A dressing area with nice shower gave us plenty of room. We had to shoo away a Vervet Monkey that came in through the sliding glass door. We had purchased fruit and cereal, coffee and biscuits (cookies) so we could have a few meals in our room when we didn't go to the camp restaurant.

In search of Wi-Fi, we drove south to **Mopani Camp** one day and had lunch overlooking the beautiful Pioneer Dam where Elephants came to drink and Hippo grunted their greeting. To enter the restaurant, we had to apply hand sanitizer and have our temperature taken. Hands-free hand sanitizer dispensers were everywhere in Africa, and our hands always felt dry. Although they claimed to have Wi-Fi at this Rest Camp, Joe was unable to connect—yes, we were in Africa.

Another day we drove north to **Punda Maria Camp** and through the **Pafuri** sandveld (sand-"felt") region with green-barked Fever Trees (so-called because they grow in malaria areas) and distinctive Baobab trees. The Limpopo River marks the border to Zimbabwe and Mozambique here at Crook's Corner. There were many folks eating at the Pafuri Picnic Site. Flushing toilet facilities (paper this time) were there, and when Jan shut the door it locked—she could not open the door! So, she loudly yelled, "Help!" several times hoping Joe would hear her. He did not, but a camp-staff man did, and he came and let her out. Adventure in Africa.

> *Pafuri - This area is certainly the wildest and most remote part of the Park and offers varied vegetation, great game viewing, the best birding in all of the Kruger, and is filled with folklore of the early explorers and ancient civilizations. It is well known for its fever tree forests, beautiful gorges and Crook's™ Corner, where the Limpopo and Luvuvhu rivers and three countries, Zimbabwe, South Africa and Mozambique, meet. The region is considered one of Kruger's biodiversity hotspots, with some of the largest herds of Elephant and Buffalo, Leopard and Lion and incredibly prolific birdlife.*
> 
> —https://www.bushbreaks.co.za/listing/pafuri-camp/

The wildlife is everywhere you turn in this area, so many dark bearded Nyala rams and fawn-colored ewes love this habitat. Monkeys and Baboons, Impala, Warthogs, the Black-shoulder Kite and Brown Snake Eagle were photographed.

Returning to Shingwedzi Rest Camp we saw Elephants. Lots of Elephants. We stopped on the Shingwedzi River Bridge where you can safely get out of the car. The riverbed was sandy and dry, but we watched Elephants dig holes in the sand with their trunks to find water to drink. While we were on the bridge Elephants were crossing the road, and one Elephant pulled up a road sign with his trunk and waved it around. We are always intrigued by Elephant behaviour.

Back at camp we noticed a camouflaged Rock Monitor lizard sunning on the trunk of the tree next to our porch. As the sun dipped, it slithered into a hole in the tree for the night. We were surprised it could fit in that hole.

We returned to the **Call of the Wild B&B** in Hoedspruit for one night before returning to Jo'burg the following day. It was hot and windy—couldn't believe we were cold and bundled up just a few days before. We had VIP service for our return flight to Jo'burg, as we were the only two passengers on the plane!

Warthogs outside the game fence along the highway

Sunset from the Shingwedzi River Bridge

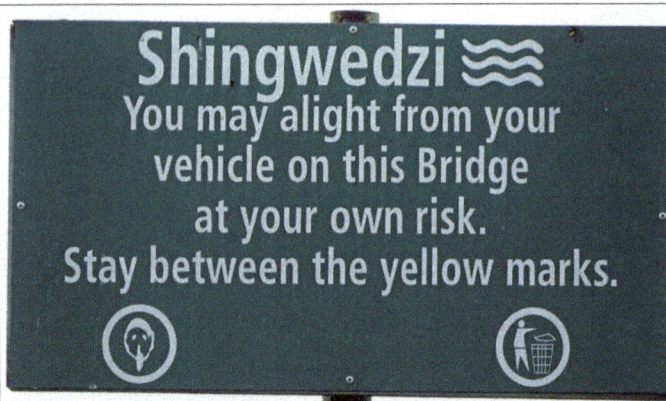

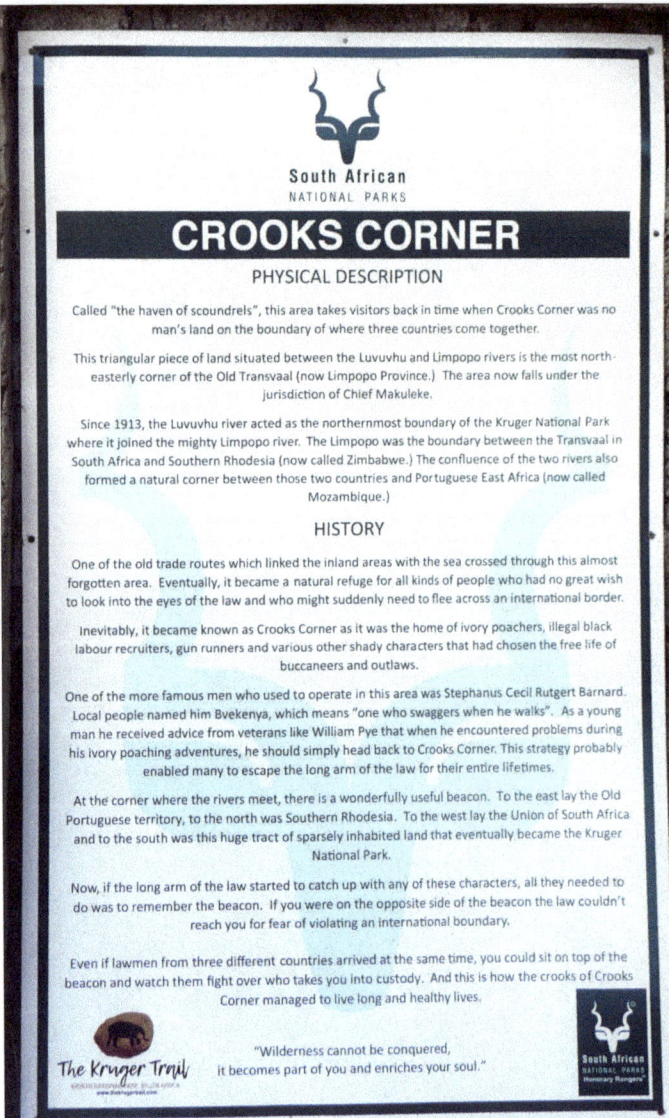

Nyala ram at Pafuri picnic site

Impala

Tsessebe

Roan

Cape Buffalo herd

Lilac-breasted Roller

Saddle-billed Storks

Male Giraffe

Baboons

Baboon with baby

Female Nyala

Male Nyala

Elephants everywhere!

Wildebeest

Black-backed Jackal

Look behind—you're being followed

Terrapins

Verreaux's Owl

Nile Crocodile

Hippo munching grass

Breeding herd of Elephants

Elephants drinking at Pioneer Dam
Mopani Camp, KNP
Hippo (below)

Elephants dig holes in sand for water to drink

Elephant plays with road sign

Sundowners

White-backed Vultures

Buffalo crossing

Juvenile Bateleur Eagle

Black-chested Snake Eagle

Black-shouldered Kite

Young female Giraffe

Water Thick-knee

Kori Bustard

Greater Blue-eared Starling

Fever trees

Baobab trees at Pafuri

Babalala picnic site

Baboon

Wooly-necked Stork

Red-billed Oxpecker on Impala

Hungry babies

75

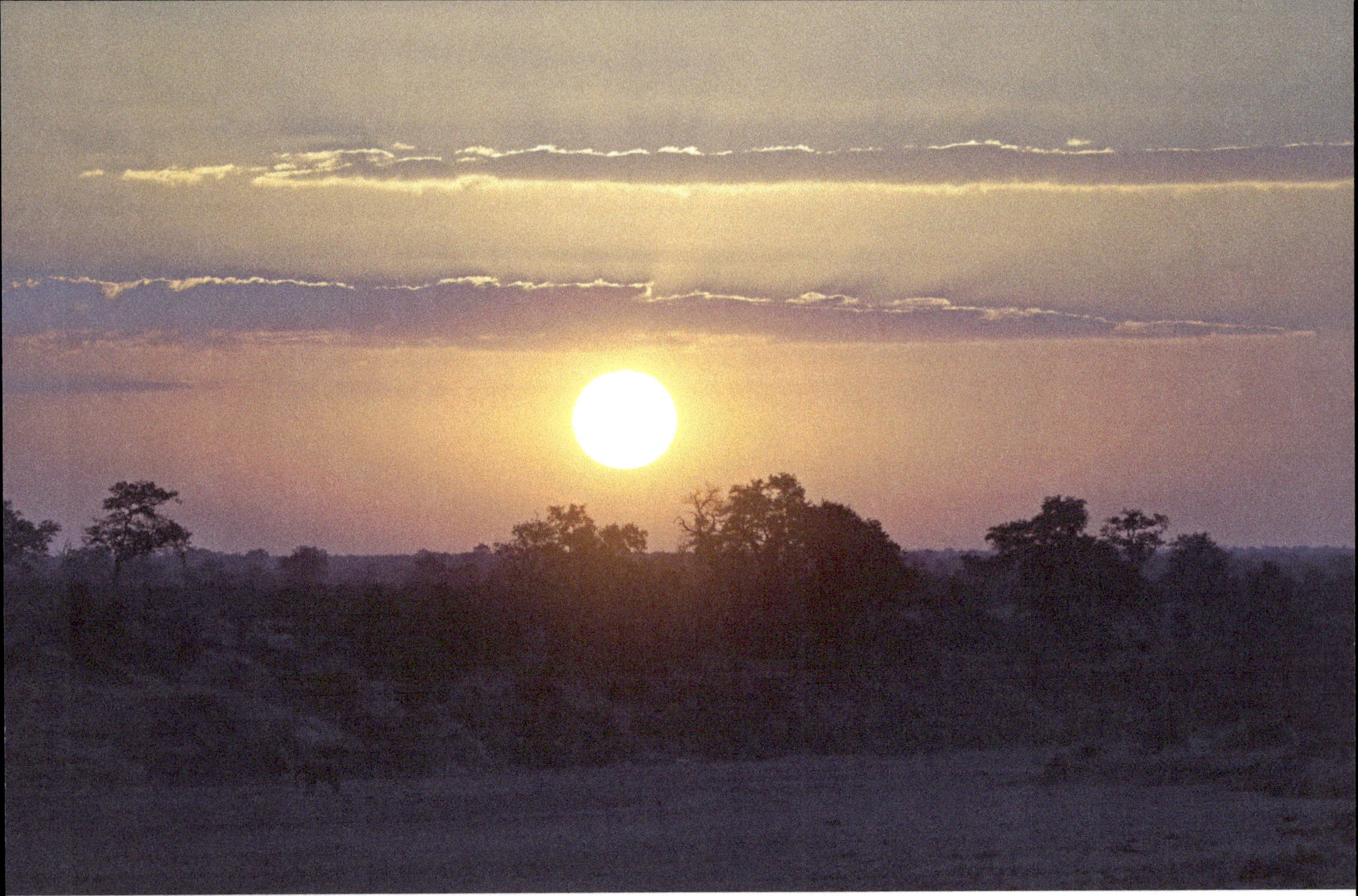

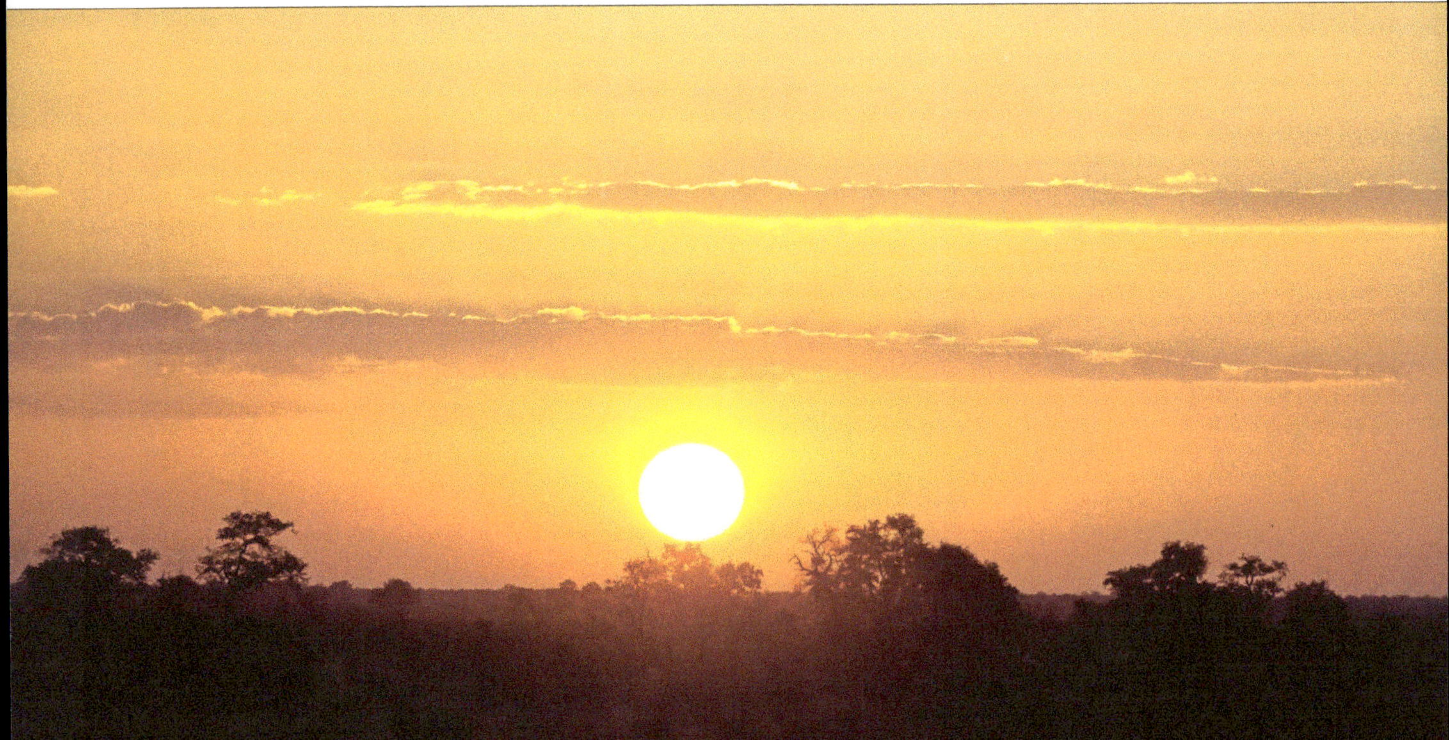

Elephant chasing Baboon

Kopje

Brown Snake Eagle

Termite mounds

Dwarf Mongoose

Crested Barbet

Giraffe chewing on a bone

African Spoonbills

Hippo (spoor) tracks

Water Monitor

Tree squirrel

Rock Monitor Lizard

Malachite Kingfisher

Setting up the trail camera
Hyena came to waterhole at night (right)

Crooks Corner Limpopo Junction, KNP

Eastgate Airport courtyard, Hoedspruit, SA

Punda Maria Rest Camp, KNP

Pafuri Picnic Site

VIP flight from Eastgate Airport in Hoedspruit to Jo'burg. We were the only passengers. View of cockpit (right)

COVID testing site at OR Tambo Int'l Airport

Airlink flight from Jo'burg to Kasane, Botswana Chobe River view from plane (right)

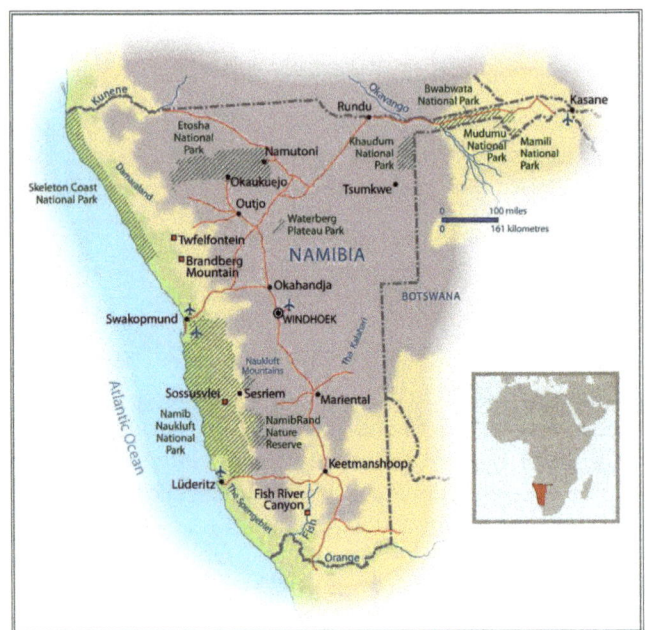

Courtesy AudleyTravel.com

# SERONDELA LODGE, NAMIBIA

Situated on the Namibian banks of the Chobe River, Serondela Lodge is facing the world renowned Chobe National Park. This will ensure all year-round close encounters with free roaming wildlife to our guest. Just 17 km (10.6 miles) from Kasane but far enough to ensure exclusivity, the guest will be part of the positive impact of sustainable tourism on this incredibly beautiful area which is situated within a very dynamic conservancy. The lodge is located in front of the renowned Serondela area in the Chobe National Park. Famous for being a major Elephant corridor as well as an area where the Lions hunt their prey.

—https://www.serondelalodge.com/

# SERONDELA LODGE

Because we were flying to Botswana the next day, we needed another COVID test... There was a testing site in the Jo'burg airport, so we paid $50 each for our tests and checked into an airport hotel. We received the negative results the next day by email. Upon arrival in Kasane, Botswana, we were quick-tested again...before clearing immigration. We had to complete entry/exit forms.

A transfer service met us at the airport and drove us into town to Botswana Immigration on the Chobe River, where we again completed exit/entry forms as we passed through. Since we had been tested for COVID twice, we boarded a boat for our next destination, two nights at **Serondela Lodge** on the **Chobe River in Namibia**. We completed exit/entry forms again at Namibia immigration across the river. We stopped frequently during the hour-and-a-half river cruise to photograph wildlife from the boat—a totally different perspective.

Serondela Lodge, an unfenced camp, has eight chalets around the main lodge with a 180-degree view toward the opposite bank of the Chobe River. The bungalow walls were constructed with sandbags and then covered with stucco. Our large room had floor to ceiling windows on two walls and air conditioning—it was hot. Double sinks were convenient in the roomy bathroom. We could not drink the water there, but bottled water was provided. We were happy to have other travelers (Italians and Germans) to visit with at this camp. It is fun to make the acquaintance with new people and share experiences.

Shortly after we arrived, Nico the guide noticed Lions on the opposite bank of the river. Agitated Baboons were barking loudly and had climbed into the tall riverbank trees. We returned to the boat and crossed the river to watch the Lions and Baboons. A pair of mating Lions rested below the trees. The following morning, we again boarded the boat and slowly cruised the shoreline finding many unique birds to photograph. But during the afternoon river cruise we had another amazing sighting.

The Lion pride had moved to a different area and were lying on the sandy shore. We watched as a young bull Elephant approached them flapping his ears with his tail straight out—chasing the Lions away! A small herd of Elephants had come to the river near the boat with their trunks raised to smell us; they wanted to cross the river. But they turned away and joined the young Elephant chasing the Lions. We waited upstream as the Elephant herd returned to the river, and once the matriarch gave the signal (how we don't know), they entered the water one by one. They crossed to the other side in single file and disappeared into the tall grass. They were two-toned as they left the water and quickly dusted themselves, sucking up sand with their flexible trunks and spraying it over their backs.

We had sundowners on the hill overlooking the river as we watched the setting sun turn from gold to orange to red, reflecting on the water, and the sky a rainbow of color. Only in

Africa could we experience such an afternoon. The frogs began their nightly chorus as we returned to the lodge for another scrumptious dinner on the veranda.

Kasane, Botswana Immigration

Boarding boat for Serondela Camp with Nico

Namibia Immigration on Impalila Island

Serondela Lodge
on the north bank of the Chobe River

Water Monitor

Pied Kingfisher

Crocodile

Yellow-billed Stork

African Fish Eagle

African Skimmer

Elephants on the Chobe River

Impala

African Darter

African Fish Eagles

Chacma Baboons in tree above Lions

Saddle-billed Stork and Great Egret

Baboon

White-throated Swallow

93

Lion - mating pair

Morning coffee before boat cruise

Hippo churning up the river

Elephants wait to cross Chobe River

After they cross, they are two-toned

Finally, a sand bath

Lions on the riverbank before an Elephant chased them away

White-browed Coucal

Lesser Striped Swallow

Malachite Kingfisher

Nile Crocodile

Green-backed Heron

Fishermen's mokoros

Kudu bull

Vervet Monkey

Giant Kingfisher

Kudu drink on the Chobe River

Water Monitor

Sundowners at Serondela

Sunset on the Chobe River

Sunset at Serondela

# CHOBE NATIONAL PARK, BOTSWANA

Aptly and fondly known as 'The Land of The Giants,' Chobe National Park in the north of beautiful Botswana is home to Africa's largest Elephant population and comprises more than 10,000 square km (3,860 square miles) of rich ecosystems, diverse landscapes and an almost unparalleled abundance of wildlife and birdlife all centered around the stunning Chobe River, and near a number of Southern Africa's other safari must-sees. Chobe National Park sits in close proximity to the borders with Zimbabwe, Zambia and Namibia, making it a popular and easy day trip destination for visitors from Victoria Falls as well as for those on tours throughout the wider region of southern Africa.

Chobe is surely the best place in Africa to see Elephants, particularly in the water. Individual herds sometimes number in the hundreds and there are an estimated 120,000 Elephants in total in the park. There are equally large herds of Buffalo to be found. In fact, both can often be seen outside the park boundaries wandering around the outskirts of Kasane itself, unperturbed by traffic or people. The Park also offers great Lion and Leopard sightings, while the river has an unbelievable abundance of Hippos and Crocodiles and an almost inconceivable wealth of birdlife, including a number of particularly rare species that are highly sought after by top wildlife photographers. This is just a small glimpse of what Chobe has to offer.

—https://www.chobenationalpark.com/

Botswana

# CHOBE NATIONAL PARK

It was quite windy for our early return to Botswana the following morning. We stopped again at Namibia's immigration (we had already completed the necessary forms), but when we arrived at the Botswana shore, we were told we would have to quarantine for twenty-four hours because we had not been tested for COVID19 before entry into Botswana. So, we paid and were tested again. We were given transport to our accommodation by a kind tour operator who happened to be there and heard our plight.

Fortunately, **Chobe River Cottages** allowed us to check in early for our three-night stay. The property owner came to see us and offered to buy some groceries and pick up a pizza for our lunch—paid from their petty cash as we had not had an opportunity to get Pula, the local currency. We were not allowed to "leave our room" during quarantine.

When planning this trip, Joe added a day here and there for contingencies such as this. We also had a flight cancellation earlier (Jo'burg to Hoedspruit), which we only learned about the night before traveling, and had to change our plans upon arrival in Jo'burg. Wi-Fi is not always available in Africa which can complicate plans. In this case, we had scheduled to pick up a rental vehicle the afternoon we were quarantined, so it was important to contact the rental company and modify those arrangements.

We had stayed at Chobe River Cottages in Kasane, Botswana before and were very comfortable in our three-room cottage. We had a full kitchen, lounge with TV and air conditioning, bedroom and a large, covered porch with table and chairs overlooking a small plunge pool. Wi-Fi was available which was a bonus.

With negative test results in hand, which were picked up the following morning by a tour company (the one we had planned to take the day before), we joined an Italian couple we met at Serondela for a Land Cruiser drive through Chobe National Park. The previous day's tour included lunch in the bush, but we were refunded for lunch since the other couple had a flight to catch that day. Serondela handled the change of plans for the tour for us. As we mentioned, tourism is very important in Africa, and personnel are very gracious and accommodating.

That afternoon we picked up our Toyota 4-wheel drive HILUX rental and self-drove the remainder of our stay this trip. **Chobe National Park** roads are <u>not</u> maintained and are often narrow dirt ruts or deep sand, so 4-wheel drive is a necessity. Due to the pandemic, there were very few other vehicles in the park. Some tourist Land Cruisers carried only one couple when they would normally seat eight to nine people.

In Chobe National Park we drove for hours without encountering another vehicle. But we did see Zebra, Kudu, Elephants, Giraffe, Sable, Hippo, Roan, and Lion. We searched for a Leopard and her two cubs another driver had told us about, but we didn't find them. Drivers often wave down other vehicles to share news of a sighting nearby. There were also Buffalo, storks, birds, Crocodile, and hundreds of Impala. We got stuck in deep sand once, but Joe was able to back out.

Our final three nights were spent at **Mwandi View Self-Catering and Lodge** overlooking the Chobe River floodplain, about an hour tar-road drive west from Kasane. This was the second time we had stayed in this self-catering camp which has camp sites, swimming pool, and restaurant with a spacious deck overlooking the waterhole. Our large elevated en-suite tent had a fully equipped kitchenette on the deck facing the floodplain. It had a small refrigerator, microwave, kettle and basic cutlery and crockery. Wi-Fi was supposed to be available from 6 p.m. to 6 a.m., but it was slow and unreliable. We eventually learned hot water was on the right in the shower…

Other tourists were in camp, and we enjoyed visiting and having a meal with a family who shared their personal bar with us. All alcohol sales were restricted in Botswana due to the pandemic—another blow to the tourist industry. We found people interested in hearing about Colorado, and they enjoyed seeing Joe's wildlife photo-book, *Finding Wildlife in Colorado.*

The next day we drove back to Kasane for the PCR COVID test required for our return to the US. We would pick up the results on our way to the airport.

We then returned to Chobe NP, and on the river road we again encountered deep sand. This time we were really stuck—up to the floorboard of the truck. It is best to lower the tire pressure before driving on the sandy roads in Chobe, and we had not yet done that, but the sand was so soft and deep even that may not have prevented us getting stuck. It was just after noon and the sun was high and hot. Joe let air out of the tires, and we tried to dig out with our hands to no avail. The sticks Jan gathered to put under the wheels were of no use. Eventually we phoned the park gate (we had our handy map and guide with the phone number), and they promised to send help. Where were we? We weren't quite sure but gave a general description of where we were headed.

An hour later Jan waved at a truck that appeared on the road above us. The driver asked if we were stuck and came down to the river road to help us. She almost got stuck, too, but had rubber traction belts which we put under her tires so she could back away. She said she would advise other vehicles where we were and went on her way. Another hour passed…we had water and food with us so we could survive, so we sat with the doors open and waited. Joe phoned again and was told help was on the way.

Around 4 p.m. a lodge vehicle came down to the river road, on a more secure surface, and assured us they would not leave us there. That was comforting since we had not seen another vehicle. Did we have water? Did we have a tow rope? A few minutes later two Land Cruisers arrived with several park people who used shovels to dig away the sand. A chain and tow rope were attached between our truck and a Land Cruiser, and they pulled the HILUX out of the sand. Joe generously tipped our rescuers. They told him they worked for a Government Agency and have performed this service many times. We thanked everyone and exchanged contact information with the lady from the lodge and were on our way. Another African adventure!

That night we enjoyed a steak dinner with our new South African friends and Amelia and Anton, owners of Mwandi View. It was a jovial dinner party, and we told the tale of our afternoon adventure in the deep Chobe River sand!

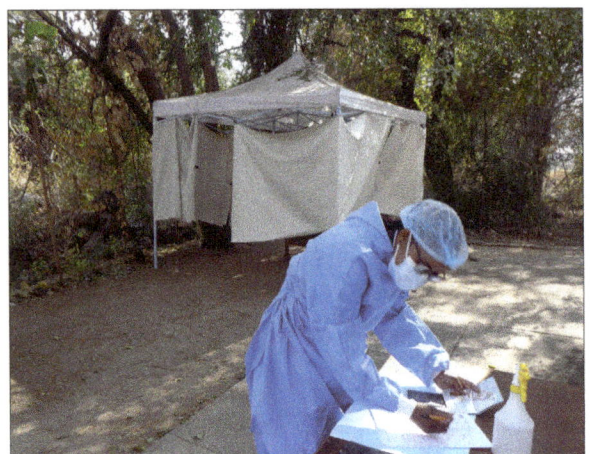
COVID testing at Botswana Immigration

Chobe River Cottages

HILUX 4x4

View of Chobe River from Chobe National Park

Kudu bull

Vervet Monkey

Big Elephant ears

Giraffe "dancing"

Zebra and foal

Warthogs

Baboons on road

Bushbuck ram

Great White Pelicans

Elephant and calf

Sable

Lioness

White-backed Vulture

Impala, Giraffe, and Kudu on the floodplain

Signs in Chobe National Park

Mwandi View tents and lounge

Mwandi View tent - view from the lodge (below)

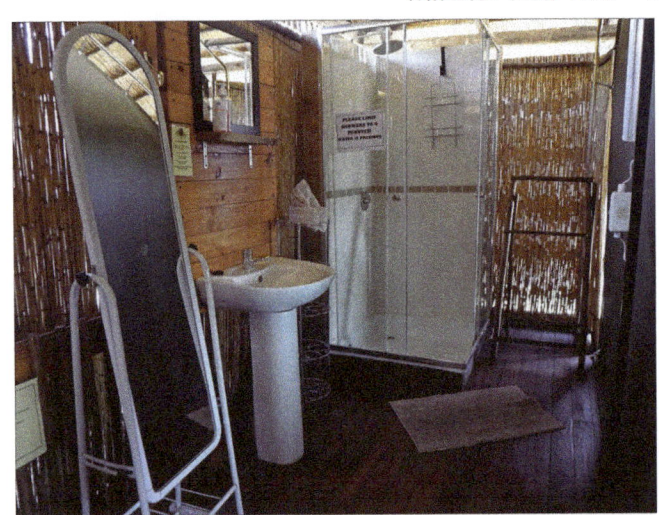

Elephant

Elephant and Impala

Stuck in the sand on the river road until help arrives to dig and pull us out

Roan

Mwandi View sunset

# SAVUTI, CHOBE NP

Savute (Savuti) is a vast open grassland famous for massive herds of Buffalos and Elephants and for the large prides of Lions that have learned to hunt them. The area plays host to dramatic scenes during the dry season when Elephant breeding herds have to drink from the dwindling surface water, and Lions ambush the young and ill members of the herd.

The lifeblood of this western section of Chobe National Park is Savute Marsh, a relic inland lake now fed by the erratic Savute Channel.

The channel is fed seasonally with water from the Kwando and Okavango Rivers, but often dries up for many seasons, probably due to tectonic plate movements, and is also thought to flow both ways on occasion.

Wildlife includes four of the Big Five (Lion, Leopard, Elephant and Buffalo – only Rhinos are absent), many antelope species, Zebras and Giraffes with good populations of Cheetahs, Hyenas and Wild Dogs, as well as a plethora of smaller species such as Serval, Aardwolf, Pangolin, Aardvark and Bat-eared Fox. The area is home to a number of large old bull Elephants as well as breeding herds that roam the area. Lion prides and Hyena clans grow to large sizes, and large herds of Zebra and Buffalo graze the extensive grasslands.

—https://travel.africageographic.com/destinations/botswana/savute-chobe/#information

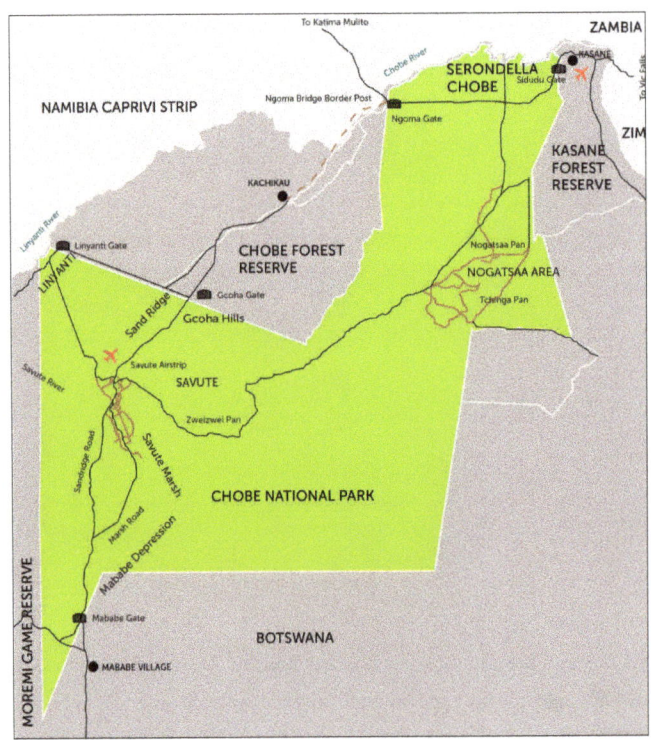

# SAVUTI

Before dawn the next morning (5:45 a.m.) we left Mwandi View for the two-hour drive, sandy roads again, to **Savuti**, an area well known for Lions and Elephants. We brought along Bogosi Kakambi (BG), to guide us there and around the area. BG, owner of **Moonlight Safaris**, was our camping safari tour operator in January 2020, when we had camped in this area. We had the tire pressure adjusted and "put foot" when we encountered deep sand stretches of the road. It was a rough ride as we bounced along rock studded roads, washboard grooves and roller-coaster hills. BG said that was an "African massage." We brought along breakfast (cereal, fruit, coffee, and a box of full cream long-last milk) and Mwandi View provided a packed lunch for us.

Soon after we entered the Ghoha Gate, we saw Lions in a quarry. They ran, but to our delight they perched on top of the hill next to the road looking down at us. The pride included seven adults (that we could see) and four fuzzy cubs. It was a great photo opportunity! Later we met with a vehicle whose driver told us about Lions on a Buffalo kill from earlier that morning. BG knew how to get to the kill and drove us there. When we approached, there were many vehicles surrounding the large pride feeding on a mature Buffalo in the middle of the road. It was an amazing sight as we watched Lions snarling at one another and vying for position to get their share of the prize. Some were enormous males. We were told this was the Savuti Marsh Pride of about twenty-five Lions. We couldn't see all the Lions. Some with full bellies were lying down in the thick bush among the vehicles surrounding the kill.

It was a windy day, so the wildlife was scarce, but we did encounter a few Elephants. When we were in Savuti eighteen months before we had seen more Elephants than we could count, but even the waterholes were abandoned this day. We did find four bulls putting on a show at a waterhole for a group of tourists having a picnic lunch. The stark white linen tablecloths and uniformed staff created quite a contrast in the bush.

BG & Joe having picnic breakfast

Lions

Lion feeding on Buffalo kill

Lion pride feeding on Buffalo kill

Tour group has picnic with Elephants at Rhino Vlei, Savuti

Picnic

Lilac-breasted Roller

Savute International Airport

Banded Mongoose

# RETURN HOME

On the return to Kasane to pick up our negative COVID test results, we stopped to watch a long parade of mothers and young Elephants cross the tar road. Such a beautiful farewell to the land we love.

Before heading to the airport, we visited Bogosi Kakambi at his home in Kazungula Village. BG and Joe spent some time in BG's office discussing some marketing ideas. His tour business (Moonlight Safaris) had been brought to a stop because of the COVID pandemic. We went down the street for a few blocks to try and get a look, from a distance, at the newly opened Kazungula Bridge over the Zambezi River from Botswana to Zambia. BG's three-year-old son Knowledge came with us.

At last we said our goodbyes and returned the truck to the Kasane International Airport, where we took an Airlink flight to Jo'burg. We had a masked four-hour layover with no Wi-Fi in the Johannesburg (O.R. Tambo) Airport. Finally we boarded a full overnight flight back to Newark, and then to Denver the next morning. Another memorable trip.

As we took off from Kasane, Botswana to return to the USA Joe took a photo of the new Kazungula Bridge connecting Botswana and Zambia across the Zambezi River. Construction was begun in October 2017 and completed in December 2020. Officially opened in May of this year, the bridge replaced the old Kazungula Ferry which had been a bottleneck for road transport and commerce for many decades. This is where the borders of four countries come together. The left side of the photo is (approx.) north and the river flows east toward Victoria Falls into the top right corner of the photo. The bridge is 3,028 feet (923M) in length.

Each visit to Africa is different in so many ways depending on the season and the weather. But the wildlife and birds are there, the sunrise and sunset color the sky aglow each day, and the hospitality is warm and welcoming. We always hope each trip won't be our last to this amazing continent.

Kasane International Airport

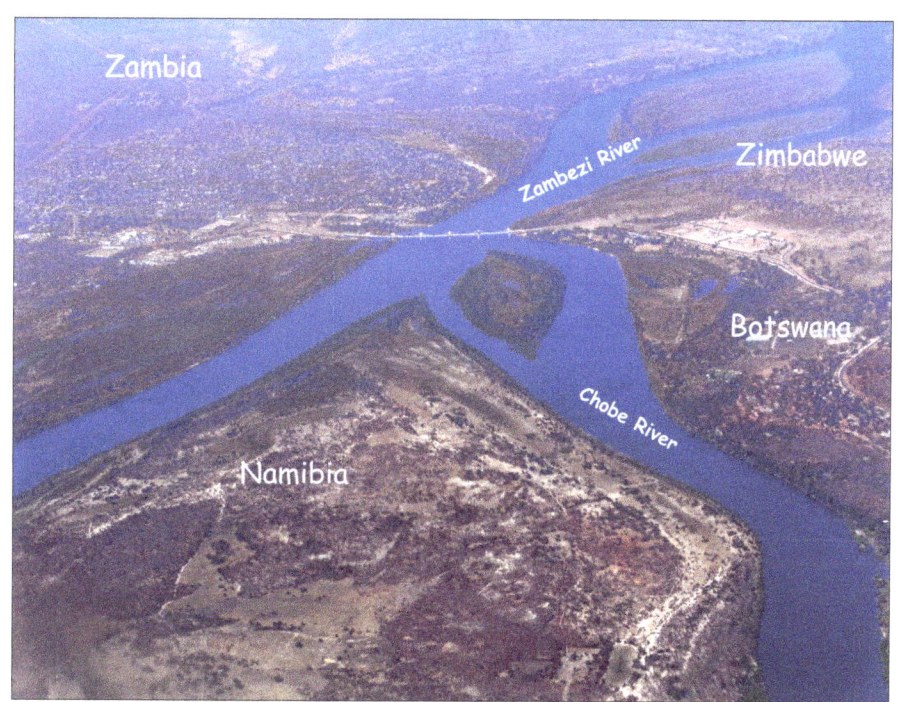
New Kazungula Bridge linking Botswana and Zambia

New York skyline from the Newark Airport Terminal

Parade of Elephants cross highway to Kasane

Bogosi Kakambi (BG) at dinner with Jan and Joe

BG's home and office (below)

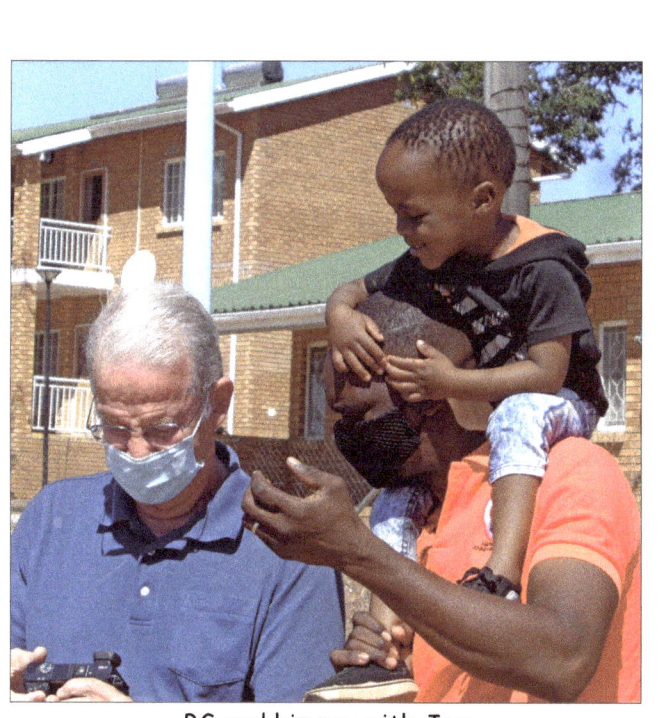

BG and his son with Joe

Neighborhood children pose for picture

"While a trip to Africa wasn't on our list of 'things to do,' before Joe and Jan invited us, it certainly is now. It is difficult to describe the awesomeness of the diversity of wildlife, people, and terrain in this beautiful country (South Africa). From a pride of Lions at a fresh kill of a mature Giraffe, to spectacular mountains and canyons, a place surfers claim produces the 'perfect wave,' the most colorful and interesting birds and flowers we've ever seen, whales bearing their young, and a diverse culture from African tribal ritual to modern cities and industry, this trip can truly be described as 'the opportunity of a lifetime.' We are thankful they invited us, and that we chose to go along. If you've never considered going to Africa...you should."

-Jerry and Joni Lund, Crested Butte CO

"We've traveled all over the world, but our trip to Africa was the very best."
-Dick and Sheila Kinsman, Littleton CO

I WAS AMAZED by the beauty of Botswana teeming with wildlife. My most memorable moments were:

- Smelling the young Elephant's breath when he trumpeted to us!
- Being serenaded by Hippos during dinner on the first night of camping;
- The breathtaking night sky;
- Spotting Spotted Hyenas and hearing them chomping on their prey behind the bushes;
- The perils of black cotton soil;
- Timoth's freshly baked bread;
- Thousands of Brown-veined White Butterflies in Moremi and Khwai;
- The tranquility of the mokoro trip;
- The helpfulness of fellow travelers to fix our flat tire;
- The Lions of Savuti and their evening lullabies!
- A herd of Elephants huddling around a young Elephant so that it could rest;
- Wild Dogs and the Lioness!
- Viewing herds of Elephant at the river's edge from the water;
- Hearing a Lion roar as we made our way out of Chobe Park on the last day of the safari. With 15 minutes to spare before the park closed and BG's expert maneuvering of the truck, we took turns to catch a glimpse of a majestic Lion through a clearing in the brush.
- Being showered by the "smoke that thunders" of Victoria Falls;
- The many laughs, awe-inspiring, and sometimes heart-stopping moments shared with a wonderful group!

What an incredible trip!

—Natalie Hirsch, Toronto, Canada

"All I wanted to do was get back to Africa. We had not left it, yet, but when I would wake in the night I would lie, listening, homesick for it already."
—Ernest Hemingway (American author and journalist)


"They say an elephant never forgets.
What they don't tell you is, you never forget an elephant."
—Bill Murray (American actor, comedian, and writer)

Africa smiled a little, when you left. "We know you," Africa said. "We have seen and watched you. We can learn to live without you, but we know we needn't yet." And Africa smiled a little, when you left... "You cannot leave Africa," Africa said. "We are always with you, there inside your head. Our rivers run in currents in the swirl of your thumbprints; our drumbeats counting out your pulse; our coastline the silhouette of your soul." So Africa smiled a little, when you left. "We are in you," Africa said. "You have not left us yet."

Anonymous

## SA/Namibia/Botswana Schedule – 2021

| Date/day | Place | Accom | Flight Lv | Flight Arr |
|---|---|---|---|---|
| Jul 24 Sat | Dep. Denver | travel | UA749-188 13:50<br>UA188-20:45 | 19:41 (EWR) |
| Jul 25 Sun | Jo/burg SA (JNB) | Aviator Hotel | | 17:45 |
| Jul 26 Mon | JNB to HDS | | FL890 11:40 | 12.35 |
| Jul 26 Mon | Hoedspruit | Call of the Wild | Bidvest Car Rental | |
| Jul 27 - 31 Tues - Sat | | Shindzela Camp – 5 nights | | |
| Aug 1 Sun | Phalaborwa | Bothabelo | AVIS | |
| Aug 2 - 5 Mon -Thurs | KNP | Shingwedzi – 4 nights | AVIS | |
| Aug 6 Frid | Hoedspruit | Call of the Wild | AVIS | |
| Aug 7 - 8 Sat - Sun | Jo/burg SA | Garden Crt Hotel | HDS FL889 14:30 | 15:25 |
| Aug 9 - 10 Mon - Tues | Kasane (BBK) | Serondela Lodge Namibia | FL306 11:40 | 13:25 |
| Aug 11 Wed | Kasane | Chobe River Cottages | ATI/Europcar (5 days) | |
| Aug 12 Thurs | Kasane | Chobe River Cottages | ATI/Europcar | |
| Aug 13 Frid | Kasane | Chobe River Cottages | ATI/Europcar | |
| Aug 13 - 16 Frid - Mon | Kavimba | Mwandi View (3 nights) | ATI/Europcar | |
| Aug 16 Mon | BBK - JNB | | FL307 14:00 | 15:45 |
| Aug 16 Mon | JNB - EWR | | UA187/2444 20:20 | |
| Aug 17 Tues | Arr, Newark (EWR) | | | 05:45 |
| Aug 17 Tues | Denver (DEN) | | 08:20 | 10:30 |
| | | 16Aug | JNB - EWR | UA187 | EWR 05:45 |
| | | 17Aug | EWR - DEN | UA2444 | DEN 10:30 |

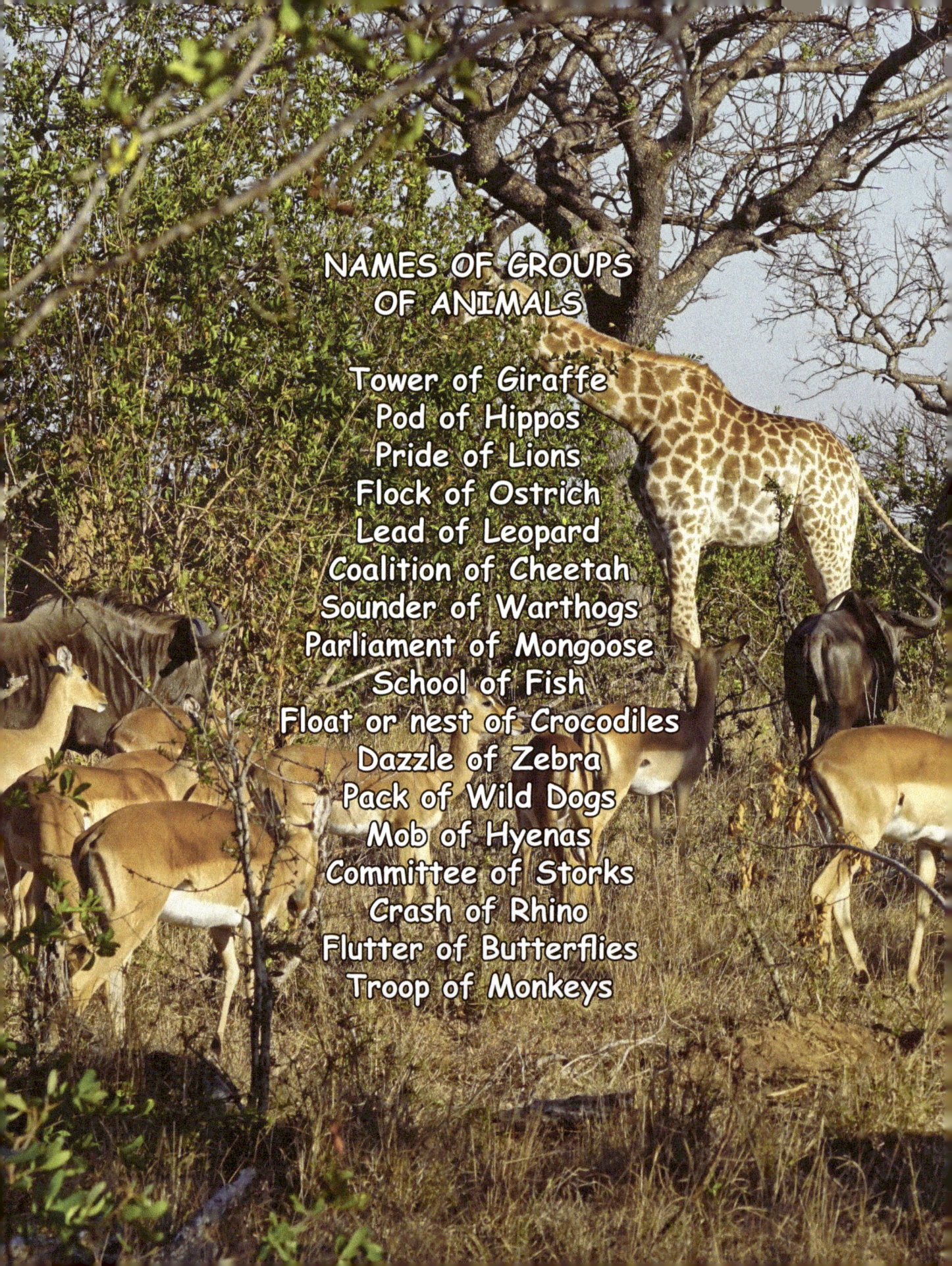

Luvuvhu River, Kruger National Park

Shindzela lounge dining area

Savuti Headquarters

This Old House Restaurant, Kasane

# About the Authors

Joe and Jan McDaniel have traveled together to Africa many times over twenty-five years. They have visited Botswana, Namibia, South Africa and Zimbabwe numerous times, often returning to private game camps they enjoy, or exploring territory they have never seen before. On most trips they rent a vehicle and self-drive when not staying in a private safari camp. Although they love to travel alone, they are Certified International Tour Guides and have escorted groups or family and friends on several occasions.

Because Joe lived in southern Africa for twenty-five years, he is well informed about the African culture as well as places of interest, national parks, and scenic landscapes. He is a zoologist and very knowledgeable about wildlife. Joe plans their trip itineraries and often makes all the bookings online. Occasionally he has worked with travel agents.

Upon return from each trip, they publish a travel journal like this one—sometimes just for themselves to enjoy and to remember a particular destination. Joe is an award-winning photographer, and what better way to preserve and share photos of a trip than in a book with text describing the activities and sights? Some of their travel books are for sale online, and several videos are available on Youtube and Rumble.

Joe and Jan own and operate BookCrafters (www.bookcrafters.net), a home-based publishing company. They assist authors who want to self-publish a book (memoir, novel, self-help, religious, photography, genealogy, family holiday, etc.).

You may reach them at bookcrafterscolorado@gmail.com.

# Other books by the author

Other books by Joe McDaniel, available from online bookstores

*Namibia Discovered* - 2018   ISBN 9781943650286

*Tallman Gulch Trail* - 2020    ISBN 9781950647682

*Finding Wildlife In Colorado* (Hardcover) - 2021  ISBN 9781950647774

*Finding Wildlife In Colorado* (Softcover) - 2021  ISBN 9781950647729

# Helpful websites for reference

https://www.Expertafrica.com

https://www.Safari.com

https://www.ati-adventures.com

https://www.audleytravel.com

https://www.serondelalodge.com

https://www.callofthewildlodge.co.za

https://www.shindzela.co.za

https://www.sanparks.org

https://www.mwandiview.com

https://www.choberivercottages.com

https://www.timbavati.co.za

https://www.moonlightchobesafaris.com

www.ingramcontent.com/pod-product-compliance
Lightning Source LLC
LaVergne TN
LVHW071955080526
838202LV00064B/6756